D1240618

So Your BITCH *is* PREGNANT

So Your BITCH is PREGNANT

Raising Your First Litter of Puppies
From **Pregnancy** to **Placement**

by Eleanor Green Winters

Front cover design by Jeff Borden.
Back cover design by Eleanor Green Winters
and Bo von Hohenlohe Productions.
Book production by Bo von Hohenlohe Productions.
ISBN-13: 978-0-578-43781-1
ISBN-10: 0-578-43781-3
Library of Congress Control Number: 2018915098

Eleanor Green Winters
Goleta, California
www.SoYourBitchIsPregnant.com

Dedication

This book wouldn't have been written without our Dennis Sanders. His mentorship was paramount in "doing it all the right way."

Dennis' example of loving kindness and practical help covers each puppy from birth throughout, encompassing the new owners as well. He is a living example of offering help and vital interest, "being there" when needed for all of us and for each pup for life!

Thank you, Dennis, for this delightful journey. I only hope that each of you will find such a dear friend and guide.

Preface

Are you panicked, thinking: "What's going to happen? What do I need? I've never even seen puppies being born, let alone raising them and finding homes!"

There is a ton of information on whelping "out there," huge tomes on birthing puppies filled with scary details, most of which you don't need to know. Having a litter of puppies is not rocket science. The process is an instinctive and natural event for your momma-to-be even if it is a big unknown for you.

There are just a few things you need to know and not much more you need to buy.

This little book is a practical overview on having a first (or even second) litter, based on my experiences of having birthed, raised and successfully placed 17 litters. With each set of pups I learned an easier way to do things.

May I share some basic tips to make this wondrous journey even more enjoyable?

Contents

Introduction

"Write the book first and the title will come to you," my daughter said. She wrote a complete novel so I listened, sort of.

Not being ready to accept her good advice, I played with two titles. Both were unacceptable.

The first was Litters Made Easy. It was good in that both litters and easy are in the title, but boring. Sounds like another self help book. Plus, when you have to make something easy you know it's probably hard in the first place.

Dismiss.

Instead of the hackneyed Litters made Easy, I toyed with another loser title, the obscure The Forever Kiss of Puppies. Of course, no one would have a clue about what's in the book. That dumb idea was born because I fervently want all your pups to have forever homes and I definitely want you to have a kiss experience. Kiss is really K.I.S.S. which is the acronym for Keep It Simple Stupid. My daughter also suggested that I take my own advice and kiss that title goodbye.

Dismiss.

I was bemoaning my lack of title while out to breakfast with my friend Rick Goodfriend (yes, that is actually his name). We laughed at both dismissed titles. When I skipped to my opening sentence, he exclaimed, "There's your title!"

So thanks to Rick I had my illusive title and could get down to writing. Thank you my good friend (I had to say that).

Dilemma solved.

Your sweet girl is going to be a momma. Canine birth and nurture are natural processes. The process can be relatively easy or complex.

It is all up to you.

My goal is to share tips that make the entire puppy experience easier for you.

Chapter 1

So Your Bitch Is Pregnant

So your bitch is pregnant.

In dog-world vernacular the correct term is bitch. Males are dogs. Females are bitches. As you undoubtedly know, the swear phrase "damn son of a bitch" means you are calling the cursee's mother a dog, a female dog, just like "doe a deer a female deer."

Whether your bitch is in an unexpected tryst "Oh no. How did this happen? She was out only ten minutes," or a planned "They had a ten-minute tie on the fourteenth day of her heat cycle," you are going to have a litter. In about 63 days! Or not. See Chapter 4 Pregnancy Midpoint as it is easy to be fooled.

If your lady's pregnancy is an "oops," don't feel too dumb. One of the first encyclopedic books on dogs states "When your female is in heat, lock the doors and board up the chimney. Even then the inevitable happens." That's not an exact quote, but you get the idea.

I have had Dalmatians since I was ten years old, many named Pepper. When my first Pepper was in season, there would be four or five of males waiting outside for Pepper's potty break. One night a little black Cocker from up the street, a persistent devil, somehow got inside the house through an open basement door and made his way through the house and up to the second floor. He was whining and scratching at his love's bedroom door where I slept in my bed next to Pepper. He didn't get her that night, but he did later.

That Cocker/Dalmatian union produced short-haired darlings ala Dalmatian but instead of spots, the pups were marked like Pinto horses with large areas of black. One even had white pantaloons. That was back in the olden days when dogs ran free in the neighborhoods. Few owners neutered their males or spayed their females. Prevention is slightly easier now due to widespread sterilization practices. Leash laws also help prevent random breeding.

With my own history of an unplanned canine pregnancy why should you listen to me? Well, I was only ten years old then and have waited some years before getting hooked again on the experience of having puppies.

At 66 I finally discovered that having puppies was by far the best job in the world. Breeding healthy, well-socialized pups for loving families adds heaps of love that I get to share. So far I have birthed seventeen litters, one litter a year, adding up to 133 puppies! I simply love having puppies. The accompanying attention is fun too. Puppy diva that I am, my love of attention is not so hidden. Puppies are love magnets. Children flock. Grumpy adults actually smile! If puppies weren't adorable, no one would gravitate toward holding and cherishing them, and by association, me. An added plus is that Dalmatians, flashy rascals that they are, have the ability to capture everyone's attention.

Not all reading this will have Dalmatians. Adjust what I recommend to fit your breed or mixed bitch. Are you used to that term yet? Bitch is so much more accurate than lady, woman, or female dog and bitch encompasses it all if you can drop the negative connotation.

But aren't Dalmatians (substitute your breed's usual characteristics) hyperactive, aggressive and mean? No. If they are bred with good temperament on top of other desirable qualities from the parents, they are wonderful family dogs. Their poor reputation comes from all the careless breeding that went on after the Disney classic 101 Dalmatians came out. Slapdash breeding will occur each time a new movie popularizes a breed in order to supply the huge demand for the darling pups. In addition, such avaricious practices totally ignore the vital, early socialization needed for the puppies. Temperament is inherited as is spotting or non-spotting, health, good movement, etc. Irresponsible over breeding of popular dogs is actually now called the "Dalmatian Syndrome."

This syndrome can happen to any breed that is movie or TV popular: Jack Russells for Fraiser, Chihuahuas after the movie Beverly Hills Chihuahua, and Rottweilers from the lovely children's book Good Dog Carl. Jack Russells are now sometimes quite hyper and may "dig to China." Rescue groups fly Chihuahuas to New England from California shelters which are overrun with these popular small dogs. Don't even mention Pit Bulls. Whether it is correct or not, Pit Bulls have a strong negative perception as does the Rottweiler. Ah, the curse of fame.

So now you are going to have the marvelous experience of having a litter! Why did I ever think that "Litters Made Easy" was a possible title? Actually I hate that made easy phrase. Made easy means that whatever you are going through is probably tough.

Not knowing what is needed as the process unfolds is hard. Puppy litters are a beautiful part of the unfoldment of life, perhaps not totally easy, but certainly joyful and natural.

Here we go. These are the tips I have learned over the years to help you to find excellent homes for your pups and to make your puppy rearing time easier. Notice that I put "find excellent homes" first. You have only eight to ten weeks minimum after they are born to rear the pups.

New parent search begins right now even before they arrive!

So Your Bitch Is Pregnant

Chapter 2

Forever Homes

Forever Homes don't just happen. You generate them. Finding marvelous parents for your babies begins right now. Tell everyone that you are pregnant!

Your bitch, however, does not have nine months. The two of you have only 63 days before the puppies arrive, remember? Anticipation can make the last month drag just like a people pregnancy. However, after the pups arrive you will have a grace period of enjoyment for about two months with the puppies. This time goes really fast.

Talk to friends, neighbors and acquaintances to get the word out that the puppies are coming. Stop people on the street. Show pictures of your darling momma-to-be. Email pictures. Tell them how sweet she is and so good with children. And her lovely temperament goes right into the puppies. Hopefully the father of your litter, known or unknown, also has a sweet disposition.

Any man, woman or child that shows a nano spark of interest goes into your contact data base to "come see the puppies after they arrive." This prospective visit is a hot combination: working on forever homes and working on socializing the puppies at the same time.

Are you overwhelmed? Don't be. Remember, for your bitch the entire process is amazingly instinctive and totally natural. For you, having a litter is unbelievably wonderful. It is scary only because the experience for you may be unfamiliar. I cannot say it enough: it is natural. Of course there is always a disclaimer: If you suspect any kind of problem, Google the subject of your concern right away and the blessed internet will help you decide the questions you need to ask your vet.

For one of my earlier litters, I vaguely remembered that I had ordered a bottle of Bitch Pills from Thomas Labs. I looked up the number of the lab on Google (I had not yet become hooked on Amazon Prime).

"Good Morning," a pleasant voice answered. "This is Jane McCormick. How may I help you?"

"Hi Jane," I replied uncertainly. "Do you carry Bitch Pills?"

Silence.

With a quizzical voice she said: "This is the Albany Seminary."

"Oh my God," I nearly said aloud, quickly adding "Oops, wrong number."

Before I finished explaining, Jane laughingly interrupted with a "Well, some of us up here may need some."

Yes, Bitch Pills are really the name! The tablets give the prospective momma the necessary vitamins and minerals to assure proper formation of the babies and also help with the nursing process. You may have to hide these pills in a meatball. I tried breaking them up and adding them to the food. Nope. There remained avoided pill chunks left in the bowl after all else was gobbled up. Bitches can be smart and selective.

I guess if it is good for us or good for our dogs, we both instinctively don't like it.

Chapter 3

Money Matters

"Why talk about money before the pups are born or even before I am sure my bitch is pregnant?"

Good question!

One answer is that many of us feel speaking about money in any situation is tactless. Another reason may be some insecurity on your part: "Maybe my price is too high?" or "I might be stuck with a pup if I charge too much?"

If you make money matters absolutely clear from the very beginning in your own mind and in the minds of your would-be puppy owners, you will have fewer problems. Furthermore, don't even consider "just giving" a pup away. There are several reasons why this is not a good idea.

The first reason refers to a non-existent or low price. Unfortunately the human mind tends to value cheaply that which is inexpensive. If we pay a higher price, we take better care of the possession. Obviously you want the very best care for your puppies. Be extra careful if you get an email that says "Do you have puppies and how much are they?" The familiar adage is that if you ask, "How much is that yacht?" you can't afford it. Don't mention price until you have recited all the things you do to assure a healthy, well-socialized pup.

The powerful biblical directive regarding low price is: "Do not cast your pearls before swine, lest they trample them under their feet, and turn again and rend you." Your puppies are the pearls and each one needs to be valued, not trampled by lack of perceived worth because of low price. Furthermore, if the inquirer claims the price is too high and he or she "can't afford" to pay that much for a puppy, how will future vet expenses be covered? The "rend" part refers to a possible character flaw in which future vet bills may be blamed on you for selling them a sick or defective pup.

You have to get to know the people that inquire about new puppies. Some people hide behind emails because they fear monetary commitment. I flat out will not deal with anyone with whom I cannot talk. Some breeders even have extensive questionnaires that each prospective owner must fill out.

The second reason not to give anyone a free or cheap puppy is also addressed in the Bible. The common sense directive "the laborer is worthy of his hire," means that someone who works should be properly compensated for the effort. You will have labored many hours and spent good money in raising your pups. That is worth something. So I repeat: do not "just give" a puppy away. Negotiate yes, but outright gift NO.

While speaking of price and expenses, I have one more (are you surprised..?) firm suggestion: get a deposit. A substantial deposit means that your potential puppy owner is serious about purchasing a pup from you. In the vernacular, he or she is not merely a "looky-loo."

My policy is to ask for a $500 deposit which will be returned any time before six weeks (when my Dalmatians receive the Baer Hearing Test) should either party have a change of mind. I always send a description of this policy so that there is something "in writing." The interested party is reassured knowing that his deposit money is not going to disappear into the ether as in a scam. If someone backs out after the six-week deadline, I keep the deposit as I may have refused others, thinking that the pup was firmly promised. The scenario of retaining the deposit happened only once in 133 puppies. The disappointed young lady with unexpected life problems actually requested that I keep the deposit!

Of course, get all the money before you release the pup. I have had a few puppy owners that I allow to make payments. So far none have disappointed me and always have come through with the total fee, sometimes a tad late, but always honored. To avoid any uncertainty you may ask for a cash payment or for a certified check. However I feel that if I haven't discovered the character of the upcoming new puppy owner by our many conversations about the pups, I deserve to be cheated if a personal check bounces.

One time a final payment was refused with a notice from my bank of insufficient funds in the new owner's account. I started to panic when I was unable to contact him. He seemed to have taken the puppy, paid me with a personal check and vanished. When I finally reached him on the phone, he had been out of town and there was a deposit mix-up on his account. He apologized and requested that I resubmit the check. It went through just fine the second time.

So I say again: make money matters clear from the beginning and you will have fewer problems.

So Your Bitch Is Pregnant

Chapter 4

Pregnancy Midpoint

At this halfway march to the birth, your only expenses have been the Bitch Pills, and any puppy toys you simply can't resist. Time to think about an ultrasound. Your bitch is already informing you about how hungry she is becoming which leads me to the next subject.

By now you are really into the pregnancy, visiting pet stores to read lists of ingredients on bags of puppy food. Nothing but the best for the babies! The expectant mother now needs a puppy dry food with high protein content, the same food you will use later when you wean the pups at three to four weeks.

About four weeks into the pregnancy, your bitch will be very hungry. I usually feed upon demand. And you can count on her reminding you of her appetite.

One morning, she may refuse her breakfast. If you are like me, that nasty feeling of guilt with the accompanying fear of vet bills jumps up.

"She's sick. Did I give her spoiled food? What did she get into? Should I take her to the vet?"

Calm yourself.

Bitches sometimes have morning sickness just like pregnant women, although crackers and soda won't work with canines. Simply pick up breakfast and save it for lunch. You can make it look appetizing by adding a spoonful of canned dog food, chunks of chicken, yogurt, anything which makes the leftover glop look better. The morning sickness will pass, usually by noon.

You both will survive.

After a litter of twelve pups when I fed my Fyrehouse Phoebe an extra meal on demand, I may have created a monster. At 8:00 every night she hovered in her feeding area demanding her bedtime meal even long after the puppies had left. She gave me a lesson in persistence.

"It's time, Mom. I want my second dinner. I will give you the stare, wag my tail and stand here until you give in."

I managed to cut the extra meal down slowly, but the habit persisted for months long after the pups had been placed. Does your girl have a stubborn streak too?

After 63 days and after expecting pups momentarily, the postman rang the bell on a Tuesday morning. He was eager to see the pups as I had told him they were due over the weekend. "I waited a couple of days like you said. Is now a good time to see the puppies?" I had asked him to wait a few days to give momma time to settle in with her babies. As this was Fyrehouse Folly's fourth litter, she was expected to be pretty calm about it all.

By that Tuesday, no puppies had been born. "No, they haven't arrived yet and I'm getting worried," I answered.

The 63 days of gestation is not written in stone and pups can come earlier or later. However, 67 days was pretty late so it was definitely time for a look with an X-ray, as Folly was quite large. I had pretty much let her have food when she "asked." Her breasts were swollen and there was even some milk in them. X-rays are deemed safe to use at the last week or so of pregancy. I had not scheduled ultrasounds with the previous three litters. Ultrasounds given at the midpoint of the pregnancy don't change the outcome, but they give you a guestimate of how many puppies your bitch may be carrying.

The X-ray taken by the vet that very afternoon showed nothing. No puppies anywhere. The accomplished three-time breeder, me, didn't even know that her bitch was not pregnant. Folly was having a false pregnancy. Because of all the hormonal changes, Folly also thought that puppies were within. Some bitches are prone to false pregnancies. I suggest you arrange an appointment with your vet for an ultrasound sometime between the 30th and 35th day of her supposed pregnancy *just to make sure.*

Bitches can fool you and themselves.

Chapter 5

Whelping Partner

You will have multiple requests to be at the birth of the puppies.

"May I be at the delivery? I have always wanted to see puppies being born." My usual answer was "No. It's not a good time for a stranger to be present." The bitch wants family for comfort, not someone new.

That refusal was automatic until Annie Scott, my neighbor, friend, and now invaluable whelping partner persuaded me to let her attend a birth. She was well known by all my bitches. Since that first birth, we have had about eight litters together and, frankly, I don't know how I survived before Annie. No help with the birthing coupled with learn-as-you-go technique is not the easiest.

Still, puppy delivery is not usually a good time for bitches to have company. My girls happily don't mind helpers or even a small, subdued audience.

The partner you pick should be a friend of your expectant momma. She should be a crazed puppy lover. If you are really fortunate, she or he will come to watch puppies being born; to hold and cuddle puppies frequently; to babysit while you run to the store; and maybe to photograph puppies. I am a terrible photographer. Annie gets right down on the floor with her phone and snaps intimate puppy moments. She's responsible for the sweet "twins" on the cover!

I lucked out with Annie. There is only one problem between us. I tend toward being cold and she toward being too hot. Keeping the pups warm is crucial. So I am comfortable while Annie suffers.

15

The ambient temperature of the room should be at least 76 to 79 degrees until the pups are relatively mobile and can easily pile up touching momma or touching each other to sleep in a cozy heap. The small size of the first bed for the mother and puppies is necessary for easy access to momma and to each other. Both the warmth of her body and the warmth of each puppy body en mass are vital. A separate pup is a cold pup.

Consulting the at-hand authority, that is the internet, I recently came across the term "shiver reflex."

Shiver reflex? You can check it out by Googling "Temperature of Newborn Puppies." The internet has excellent education on every question you may have. The good information up front is always followed by the disclaimers. It's like watching pill commercials on TV with the myriad of side effects, or watching a knee replacement video before your knee surgery. Scary.

I suggest that you invest in a good space heater. I bought one that swivels and can be set to maintain a specific temperature within two degrees. Perfect. Place it near but not directly blowing on the pups and you are all set. You know the temperature is about right if you occasionally breakout with a sweat or think you may be having a hot flash. Oops, don't mean to be sexist, but most litter caregivers are women.

As the puppies grew, Annie also played with them. While I made sure there was no poop to step in, Annie was the pups' toy and tug partner, running energetically with them around the yard. She proved the truism "A tired puppy is a good puppy" which is right up there with "Let sleeping dogs lie."

My hope for you is that you can find someone like Annie.

Chapter 6

Signs

You may notice how loving, affectionate and even clingy your bitch is becoming. In addition to hovering she may eat you out of the proverbial house and home and begin to look like a beached seal.

Or not.

Her size depends on how many pups she is carrying and how big they are. Some breeders have the skill to palpate the uterus to feel how many pups are present. I've never had that ability. Moreover, the ultrasound is not infallible as to the number of pups. What comes, comes, is my philosophy. My mantra has always been it is all natural.

When expecting her first litter, I noticed that my Folly kept appearing with a dirty nose. This was odd as she was not a digger and never buried bones. In addition to her increased affection, she was expressing another exciting sign of the coming birth. She was nesting.

You will find the beginnings of a den behind a bush, in a dark corner of the yard or in a closet where your girl has been scratching at the carpet. Usually nesting begins outside. A dirty nose is the biggest clue. Pop a large rock into the beginning den she has begun excavating or it will soon be a huge pit. Place a piece of furniture in her favorite scratching corner inside the house or fence it off. She can do all the nesting she wants in her crate, piling up her blankets into a heap. I am assuming that you crate train your dogs.

An aside: crate training is not evil or cruel. Explain to expectant owners that the crate is the pup's den, hideaway and safe spot. The biggest plus in crate training is that the pup won't chew or eat dangerous objects when you are not watching, something that may cost you a fortune to have removed surgically. In addition, crating your pup means your possessions remain secure when you leave the house or when you are not particularly alert to the endless mischief a puppy presents. The pup also feels safe and cozy in his or her space.

This nesting activity alerts you to the next job. It is time to set up the whelping box. Now also is a good time to arrange back-up help with your vet by making sure someone can be on call to answer any questions. Should you think anything might be difficult (huge pups, complex birth, very large litter) consider a Caesarian.

Jolene De Graef, my friend who owns and handles the first American Kennel Club Champion I bred, always schedules a Caesarian as she lives on a ranch about two hours from a vet. She does not want to take any slight chance of losing a pup should a problem arise.

I have been very fortunate. In seventeen litters, no Caesarians and only once a trip to the vet for help in the birth process. My bitch Fiona was fatigued after birthing ten pups and was straining unsuccessfully to push out the remaining pup. I called my veterinarian Dr. Kelly Doria who suggested I bring momma and all the pups that were born in to see her. I speedily popped all ten puppies and momma in the car. Immediately after arriving at the clinic, Dr. Doria was able to reach inside Fiona and pull out the eleventh pup uttering a surprised "It's alive!"

She then suggested taking an X-ray to make sure there were no more pups inside. We had another surprise when the X-ray showed one more pup still to be born. She promptly administered a shot to Fiona to stimulate her lagging contractions and happily the twelfth was born also alive and well.

The survival of those last two babies was a huge cause for celebration for me, for my marvelous vet and for all the office staff. At that point poor Fiona couldn't have cared less: ten, twelve, whatever. She contentedly carried on the nursing of all the puppies almost saying "What's two more?"

So Your Bitch Is Pregnant

Chapter 7

Whelping Box

Buy a hard-plastic, child-sized "kiddy" pool to use as a whelping box. I have found that the kiddy pool is the best fit for my K.I.S.S. philosophy. Remember what that means: Keep It Simple Stupid.

If you are like me, I forget the advice unless I know why:

- First, kiddy pools are cheap. However, there are many styles of whelping boxes. Certainly check them out and compare as there are many types available.

- Second, the plastic pools make for easy cleanup and protect your flooring, carpet and/or tile grout. Try to find a pool without the cutesy indentations on the bottom which collect poop.

- Third, the little rascals need to be enclosed or your stuff will be chewed, scratched and moisturized.

As for the size of the kiddy pool or whelping box, your bitch should fill one half of the area when she is lying down and stretched out. At birth the pups are totally blind and deaf. They find their mother by going to her warmth, moving like early invertebrates toward her body heat. So you want a short journey for the little guys. Make sure there is a blanket or bedspread under the whelping box you have chosen. Keeping the puppies toasty warm is crucial to their survival!

This setup will work perfectly for about three weeks. When eyes and ears are fully opened, the babies quickly learn to scramble over the edge! Invariably I find an adventuresome pup spread-eagled on the tile, whimpering at being alone and cold. This is my clue that it is time to get out the bigger pool.

Oops! Did you think one pool would take care of it? Nope. Unless you have a small breed, the pups and mom will fill up the space rapidly. Also pups manage to get over "impossibly-high" sides very quickly just like a child climbing out of a crib. They will climb onto their mother and tumble over.

Before the pups escape, buy a larger plastic pool with higher sides. Also you need to order a 24 inch X-pen to surround it. An X-pen is the helpful metal fencing that can be set up in any shape and will definitely keep them contained. To connect the ends together, purchase some Double-Headed Bolt Snaps (it took me three trips to the hardware store to remember that moniker). You can always use the fencing later out in the yard or patio. Black fencing blends into the greenery outside better than the silver. Leftover pools can go to the neighbor kids should you decide that having a litter is a never-again experience for you.

To reiterate: thus far you have had only the cost of Bitch Pills, two inexpensive plastic pools, an X-pen or two with fasteners, and maybe some high protein puppy food to feed your bitch. Oh, add the ultrasound if you decided to get one.

I lied about low expense. There is no cheap way to have pups even when all goes smoothly. Obviously with a first litter you do have initial equipment expenses. For one early litter I kept detailed records of the cost and time involved. I netted a whopping $2.35 an hour! I admit that I included several interrupted nights in the hourly count.

Having puppies is definitely a labor of love. And that's okay, as the entire experience is filled with love and joy and ongoing delight as you prepare the pups to go to their new homes.

Chapter 8

One Week To Go

You will know when it is time to set up the whelping area. The clue that pups are coming is the energetic nesting by your bitch. Yes, it is going to happen. She knows it. You know it. But where?

Many say the bitch wants a dark, secluded corner like a den. I say maybe she does, but I want convenience. My litters are born smack dab in my sitting room, open to all activity. "Get used to it girl. This is how it is going to be." The puppies will be exposed to noise and activity before they can even hear or see.

To save your back, get a wooden pallet to raise the pool. Cover the wood with an old bedspread. I admitted that a raised pool would help my back sometime after the twelfth litter. Guess I am a bit of a slow learner. Annie, my dear whelping partner, is the one who first suggested raising the pool height with a pallet and then went out and got one for me. It helped!

During this last week alert your vet and make a tentative appointment to have the pups' dewclaws removed. Dewclaw removal is usually done the second or third day after the pups are born. The dewclaws can catch and rip on decking etc. as they get older, necessitating a trip to the vet with a dog in serious pain. Early removal after their birth is like attending to a hangnail whereas later dewclaw removal is a difficult operation. Hopefully your vet is as skilled in this procedure as the vet I now have (thank you Dr. Kelly Doria!). If the nail bed is not totally removed, the pup will have a partial nail which grows out. Someone will have a nail biter in the family.

That last week before her due date put soft blankets or towels over the bottom of the pool and coax her into lying down comfortably and relaxing. At first she will resist, but persist in leading her into the pool, praising her when she lies down and rewarding her with a treat if necessary. Let her nest there and pet her. Your attitude is a firm this is where the puppies arrive. Period.

Hedge your bet on the place of arrival by having a slip leash handy. After you get tired of all the pre-contraction panting, frantic nesting and pacing which can go on for hours, her first good contraction may pop out a pup while she is still in her crate, in your closet, on your bed, anywhere inconvenient and possibly hard to reach. Slip the lead over her head, pick up the newborn pup and march both to the pool whelping box. Then she will stay put, cleaning her first baby, awaiting the next arrival.

Scared? Don't be. Remember: It is all natural. She knows what she is doing even if you don't.

I have been pretty dogmatic (pun definitely appropriate) in insisting that the birthing pool be set up for my convenience in the middle of my living space. That worked with four generations of my bitches with 16 lovely litters. The first-time momma of my 17th litter had a different idea and she won. After birthing, cleaning and feeding her pups, she would pace, whine and she even worked up a fever.

We both had two sleepless nights. On the beginning of our third night of sleeplessness when she exhibited a fever, we went to the overnight vet. Blood tests indicated that she was in excellent health in spite of the fever. They prescribed antibiotics deemed safe for nursing puppies and sent us home.

Finally it was I who belatedly realized that she was telling me "I don't care if you have had 16 litters with this setup out in the open, I won't tolerate it." That night I tried putting her in her crate in a darkened closet with her pups. The night went by without a peep. She was happy. The pups were happy. I managed a good night's sleep and I was happy.

Once again I learned something new: listen to your bitch. Throw out all preconceptions and open your mind. She will communicate what she wants.

Chapter 9

Birthing Setup

For the birth you need all of the following:
- Large towels
- Bar rags (absorbent terrycloth rags you can buy in bulk)
- Baby wipes
- Buckets (2)
- Small cardboard box or basket
- Hot water bottle
- Chairs (2)
- Heater
- Water bowl
- Scale for weighing pups (optional)
- Puppy ID ribbons or collars (optional)

Don't forget that birthing is thirsty work. Frequently offer water to the bitch. Annie and I hydrate ourselves with diet cokes and lots of them. Yes, I know. Water is better, but the diet cokes keep us awake and caffeinated for our part of the process.

Towels and bar rags are the best for all kinds of cleanup. Don't even think about newspaper to line the pool. Newsprint doesn't absorb and it covers the newborns with black grime. Paper towels are stiff and do not absorb well unless you buy the expensive, softer brands.

Don't over wash momma as the pups move toward her scent

as well as toward her warmth. Annie discovered the technique of wrapping the bitch's tail with stretch bandage tape to keep the tail clean as it is always right there where the action is going on. Cold water soaking will help launder the bar rags and towels from the birthing residue. Yes it is messy, very messy. The pool can be rotated during the birth so that you can readily reach the arriving pup, help wipe it dry, and clean up the fluids and afterbirths. It is natural that your bitch eats several of the placentas. Ugh, you say? Well, yes, but it is instinctual and part of the process.

If you choose not to sit on the floor, set up the chairs and place the small box containing the hot water bottle next to you. I suggest a box with short sides so the momma can see that her pups are safe. You can then keep a pup or two warm and out of the way while mother is busy birthing another pup.

Place two buckets within throwing range. One is for soiled rags and towels. Line a second bucket for trash with a plastic bag. A stack of clean bar rags must be within reach. Watch out for cheap bar rags as they are not absorbent until they have been washed forever.

Oops. I almost forgot. Plastic gloves are a must if you are squeamish. I don't bother with gloves for the birth process but will use them later when momma relinquishes the poop cleanup job. I like vinyl ones that fit well. I also use some talcum powder to dust my hands to make the gloves easier to put on. No one wants stuff under their fingernails. Also treat yourself to at least one Ettore 32" Grip N Grab (bless Amazon Prime) which is perfect for swishing a bar rag around the bottom of the pool to get rid of any wetness or mess. Having this tool handy will also save your back.

Buckets within throwing range? Grip and Grabs? These items are especially needed after you have been up birthing puppies all night or up those first nights checking to make sure the pups are not squished by the new momma. Trust me. You will appreciate the smallest thing that can ease your up/down work!

As for the id ribbons and a scale, I don't use them. I consider the litter a mass entity until I can identify an individual pup and give it a name. However, you can now buy colored collars with Velcro for expansion as the pups grow. The collars identify each pup by color until you can tell them apart.

Regarding weighing pups on a special scale, I feel that daily weight checks are to reassure you that all is well and that all the pups are thriving. One can usually visually spot a pup that is not gaining weight or nursing well. Then, of course, check it out online and/or with your vet. I make sure that the littlest ones get to a full breast when they are crowded out by the bigger, stronger pups.

Remember that for thousands of years pups have been born in holes in the ground without any human help. Some pups are stillborn or just don't survive. That is nature's way of saying not meant to be. None of us want to hear to that phrase. Do what you can within reason. I am counting on the best scenario for each of you! If you do have a stillborn pup, the mother seems to know it. I simply remove it quickly. My bitches accept it and get on with the rest of the litter.

You are now ready for the birth except for one more collection which I call the "Birthday Box."

Chapter 10

Birthday Box

Your Birthday Box contains items crucial to have with you on birthing day or more likely, birthing night! When my matriarch Folly had her first litter, I had no idea about most of the things needed in a birthing kit.

Now I have a small box ready for the birthday party containing:
- •Rectal thermometer and shields
- •Small scissors
- •Dental floss (for tying off the umbilical)
- •Suction bulb (small)
- •Rubbing alcohol
- •Pad and pencil
- •Puppy ID ribbons or collars (optional)

Prior to birth the bitch's temperature may drop by stages from the usual 101 degrees to 98 degrees indicating that birth is imminent. This drop in temperature is not an infallible sign of impending birth, but it is an indication. Restlessness and panting are also signs. If you use a rectal thermometer to check her temperature, definitely use thermometer shields. I didn't use a shield one time and discovered that the odor doesn't wash off.

You may want colored ribbons or collars to identify each pup. As I mentioned, I never bother with the collars. I feel that there is enough activity going on at the birth not to worry about labeling each pup. I am always concerned regarding collars getting caught on something with pups as well as with my adult dogs. In addition I don't like interim labeling of "Red Boy" or "Pink Girl." I put off naming until I can pick out individual pups and give them their special names.

The bitch does the work of chewing off the umbilical by crushing the open end with her teeth which helps to stop the bleeding. The dental floss is for tying off an umbilical cord that continues to bleed. In 133 pups, I have never had to use the floss. Let momma take care of it. If it is bleeding, it soon stops. Occasionally you may need small scissors to cut off a dangling piece of umbilical.

I didn't even know that it is perfectly natural for the mother to eat the placentas. That frantic gobbling can freak you out if you don't know it is a necessary part of the process. I usually try to stop this consumption of the afterbirth at about three to limit subsequent diarrhea in the mother.

Some breeders take the bitch within the first twenty-four hours to their vet for a "clean-out" shot in case all placenta material has not fully been expelled. I don't unless I suspect a problem with retention. As you have to drive the entire new family to the vet for dewclaw removal sometime during the first three days, I feel that an additional trip to the vet for a cleanout shot adds one more disruption to the bitch's settling in with her litter.

At that first birthing maybe I did know enough to jot down the time and sex of each pup when it was born, but that was about it. The fifth pup to arrive was having difficulty breathing, sticking his tongue out and wheezing. I tried to clear his nose but he still struggled to breathe.

I was seated on the floor in my office where the pups were being born. Just in back of me was a floor to ceiling bookcase with the bottom shelf doubling as a liquor cabinet. I reached around and grabbed the gin bottle, tipped some gin onto my finger and put my finger to the pup's mouth. He let out a shriek and breathed perfectly from that moment on. That tiny taste of Bombay Sapphire cleared all passageways instantly! Alcohol isn't all that bad. From that time on he was the loudest shrieker of the litter.

I recently discovered that the swing method to let gravity help remove mucus from the newborn's nose is not currently in favor. I also found out that I was unaware of a definite technique in using the suction bulb. Check out both methods on line.

As I began with the homegrown "gin method," I think it is wonderful that I made it this far without losing a viable pup!

So Your Bitch Is Pregnant

Chapter 11

What Ifs

I didn't want to include this chapter. Sometimes problems arise but hopefully not for you and not this litter. I have tucked several scenarios into previous chapters almost as an aside because my fervent desire is that you experience the wonder and naturalness of the entire process.

Use common sense, be aware, check the internet, and assuredly call your vet if there seems to be a problem. Of course, anything that might need assistance usually happens on the weekend or at night.

Stillborns

Stillborns happen. A fully formed pup sometimes can be born lifeless. The cause varies. So very sad.

Deformity

Only one of some 133 pups I have had was deformed. At birth a male was born with a partial right front leg. I took him to the vet the next morning expecting that they would suggest that he be put down. The vet surprised me by having me sign the pup over to them so that they could care for him until he was old enough to have the limb removed. They had a female present at the veterinarian practice that could nurse him.

The next day the vet's office called and asked if the pup could be returned to the litter as the lactating bitch they had on hand did not work out. Of course I took him back into the litter. We named him Stump. We wrapped the limb and he "swam" around with his litter mates until he was big enough for surgery at six weeks.

Stump had his operation and the leg was removed at the shoulder. By that time a vet tech that had helped with the operation had fallen in love with him and he became her dog. She lived locally so I often saw Stump at the park running with the rest of the dogs there. He would fall over and get right up and go on. His owner dropped Stump as his name and named him Bruno which I think was a marvelous overcompensation. The two of them went together to Kansas where she studied and graduated as a veterinarian.

Breed Problems

Each breed has some inherent problems. Dalmatians have deafness in the breed as do many primarily white-coated animals with light eyes. We test for deafness at six weeks.

Ayres Mitchell, a dear friend who has one of the Dalmatians I bred, has helped me with six or more litters. At six weeks we load up the puppies and drive to the vet that does the Baer Hearing Test. Of course the vet who has the specialized equipment for the test is located about two hours up the road. Ayres and I have it all down to a science with the midday stop at In-N-Out Burgers as our treat. We leave Santa Barbara early in the morning and drive at least one hour before the shrieking puppies quiet down. One time we made the trip up with no poop or vomit, put the pups out on an untraveled grass area in an X-pen, fed and watered them, had all the twelve tested, microchipped, and given first shots, ate our burgers and returned home with no accidents. That was a hugely successful day especially as all twelve had perfect hearing. In addition, the pups were all tired out from their adventure and slept quietly all the way home!

"They," the great all-knowing group, say that a mutt is a better choice health wise than a purebred canine. However, if either or both of the parents of the mongrel have problems, the pups just might inherit their problems. As the phrase goes, there are no guarantees regarding health. We try our best with hip, thyroid, eye, ear and elbow testing, but a breeder has no control once the puppy leaves. We will assuredly be there for the new owners to guide and help with questions on health, socialization and training. I have an extensive folder with a contract, feeding and training suggestions, microchip information, pedigree etc. that goes home with each pup. New puppy owners have a lot to absorb. Reiteration is the key! Many times I get questions to which I have to reply: "It is in your folder under Puppy Suggestions" or "the microchip papers you have in your folder."

Parvo

I have put off writing this chapter for weeks now because of the worst unnatural happening: the horrendous scourge Parvo, the absolute nastiest "what if." Puppies die. I have never experienced it directly in my home with a litter, thank God, but if it is in your area, you must take precautions to minimize the danger.

The immunity that the pups receive from the mother usually holds. However I command: never let the pups leave without having received the first Parvo inoculation (given at 6 to 8 weeks). If you do have Parvo in your area, have visitors use wipes on their hands and remove all shoes in the puppy room. Check with your vet for suggestions for preventive methods.

In one of my first litters I ignorantly allowed two pups to leave without their shots as the two new owners were going to the vet the very next morning. Somehow they picked up Parvo at a potty stop on the way to their new home. One pup died and one pup lived after extensive vet treatment. I still feel ghastly about these two tragedies.

To end this unpleasant chapter I have one reiterated suggestion. If you are not sure about anything talk, ask, research and get help from your veterinarian.

Chapter 12

The Pups Are Here

The halcyon days are here. You have birthed your litter. You have cleaned up the mess. Don't be too thorough in cleaning the pups or washing the bitch as the birth scent cements their bond. You have also dragged the reluctant momma outside to pee. Upon returning her to her babies, offer her more water and possibly a small meal.

In the morning (I am assuming you have had some pups arriving at night) call your vet to confirm your appointment to have the pups' dew claws removed on day two or three. Hopefully you have already made that appointment even before the birth. Most vets will make adjustments based on the actual arrival date.

You will now have about two weeks of easy delight. Everything stays relatively clean the first couple of weeks as all bitches have to lick the babies to stimulate them to urinate and defecate. Momma instinctively cleans everything up so as to remove any scent that might attract predators. Obviously we don't have predators in our house, but the "den" used to be in the forest, not in a whelping pen inside your home.

Some bitches will become upset if you have too many visitors. Your clue is seeing momma looking nervous and attempting to move the pups to a more secluded spot. She may even resume digging a den in your back yard. Back off on the visitors.

When my matriarch Folly was interestedly watching her daughter Olivia birthing her first litter, I happily thought "Isn't this delightful family togetherness." After the fourth pup was born and had been cleaned and nursed, the fifth one presented. I moved the four out of the way closer to Grandma Folly who was observing with attentiveness. Just after the fifth pup was nursing nicely, Folly looked over the pile of four tiny pups toward new momma Olivia and growled. It was like Folly was telling her daughter "Okay I will take over now."

Olivia immediately stood up, dropping the fifth pup to the floor, and made a bee line to the door to go outside, almost like she was replying "Okay mom, whatever you say. They're yours."

I had panicked thoughts of "Oh my God, I may have to hand feed the entire litter if Olivia backs out." Immediately I shut Folly into another room and dragged Olivia back into the birthing pool where she proceeded to have five more pups. She frequently checked Folly's whereabouts through the fencing I had hastily set up. After Olivia's milk came in the next morning, she finally understood that these were her pups. She eyeballed Folly and growled possessively. After that statement of intent from Olivia, all was restored to harmony in the family. I felt as though I had dodged a very big bullet. My lesson was that it is best to begin with clear separation of adult dogs and whelping mother. Later you may carefully and gently introduce the adults to the litter as your bitch permits.

In subsequent litters Grandma Folly (who was prone to false pregnancies) actually produced milk and eagerly helped nurse the pups. She would stand outside the pen and whine until I would let her in to be with the pups.

We had some very fat and happy puppies with two mothers providing milk.

Chapter 13

The Nursing Mom

You've heard the expression "Sucking hind tit." It means a paltry amount of anything. The phrase supposedly refers to mammals wherein the hind tits are smaller and produce less milk. Not true of canine bitches. Those hind tits fill up to the size of small cantaloupes.

I don't want to discuss a possible problem, but Watch her tits. Overnight they can become hot and hard indicating a beginning mastitis.

When you first catch a breast becoming large, firm and overly warm, sit with a large bowl of hot water, so hot you can barely squeeze out the washcloth, and put it over and around the breast. When it cools, stick it back into the hot water and reapply. After five or six applications, get the biggest and strongest puppy in the litter and put him or her on that tit to keep the milk flowing. I have stopped a full-blown mastitis from forming at least four or five times with hot packs followed by the expression of milk from that particular breast.

Once with my Fyrehouse Phoebe I didn't catch it. Almost overnight the infection became nasty. I was scared. The pups were just three weeks old. Of course it was on a weekend so to the overnight animal hospital we went. They kept her for two days until she somehow recovered from 106 degree temperature which can be fatal. Saving her was wonderful.

However, my instructions when I got her home were overwhelming. I was to hot pack her every three hours; to massage the still infected breast; to express milk and infection; to give powerful antibiotics with food; to keep her from nursing the pups ever again; and finally to give pain medication. In addition, I was weaning the three-week-old pups. Phoebe, in pain, didn't want to eat. I was exhausted. The phrase I am too old for this shit kept running through my thoughts. No one is young enough for the seeming endless sleepless nights. I needed help desperately.

Help came immediately when I called my angel, my dear friend Tracy Rossello, who owns the father of three of my litters.

After my cry for help, this fabulous friend jumped on the train from Oceanside, California, arriving in Santa Barbara some six hours later. She immediately assessed my stress level and took Phoebe with her to a Motel Six nearby where she nursed her constantly for three complete days, getting all that medication in her and the infection totally out. With the aid of McDonald plain cheeseburgers, she made sure Phoebe ate before receiving medication. She saved me!

She also improvised the canine version: "Just a spoonful of burger makes the medicine go down," buying three to four plain cheeseburgers daily.

Poor Phoebe could only be with the pups wearing bloomers and a tee shirt. We would suit her up and she would go in with them. They would try to nurse through the tee shirt so we would drag her away and remove all her clothing. We had to do that procedure each time she whined to go in with the pups. That dressing-undressing got very old quickly and both Phoebe and I tired of it. She never did develop a relationship with the pups of that litter. Thank goodness they were old enough to wean without hand feeding.

Phoebe and I both recovered. The following year she had a complete relationship with her twelve new pups.

So I say again: Watch the tits.

Chapter 14

Cleanliness

Momma has begun the potty training by lapping and eating the excrement. Ugh you say? Be thankful, for later she will back off from that job and the cleanup detail will be all yours.

When the poop starts to appear unclaimed by momma, remove all towels except those making a pallet at the back of the pool. At the same time, slightly elevate the back of the pool with towels or blankets. The pups will gravitate away from the nursing bed at the back toward the cleared part of the pool to eliminate. They instinctively want their sleeping area clean. The slant will mean the mess will be out front on the plastic floor of the pool where you can get at it more easily. If you are not using a plastic pool as a whelping box, elevate the back sleeping area slightly with towel pallets to help the pups recognize the "clean area."

Use a grabber with a bar rag to soak up the pee on the plastic. Use baby wipes to pick up the poop. Paper or cloth will smear the poop. You can use puppy pads for a while, but eventually the pups will begin to play and rip them. Sometimes I don't even bother. The plain plastic is easiest to clean.

If you are using a simple penned in area, consider putting a piece of artificial turf or even a rectangle of real grass sod (on plastic or in a container) at the end of the pen away from the sleeping area. In that way you can accustom the pups to pottying outside on grass while they still are inside!

Watch in amazement as the pups gradually move to potty further and further from their sleeping blankets. This actually is instinctive Potty Training 101, carefully engineered first by the bitch in her early cleaning, and advanced by your efforts at keeping the pool or pen scrupulously unsoiled.

Generally they pee when they wake up and, pretty much like clockwork, poop after eating. Of course the axiom "the exception proves the rule" still applies. Be ready to swoop and scoop with your gloved hand and wipes at the ready. Usually the desire for speed negates your taking the time to put on a plastic glove.

As you have a calm period right now before you start to wean the pups, begin thinking about preparing a second confined area for the pups. You can set up a second clean pen outside if you have good weather. At weaning two separate areas are pretty much essential for your continued sanity. Otherwise the pups will get accustomed to being "dirty" and will be difficult to potty train. New owners will say "We love this pup but we are still having accidents in the house." Not a good start in their forever homes.

In addition, you must also teach the new parents how to potty train their pup. Each time the pup changes activities in their new home, tell them to take the pup out to a spot of their choosing to eliminate. That means they go out to pee after a cuddle session, after eating anything, after a nap or possibly even after changing toys. Then owners and puppy both get to wait, wait and wait some more until success. If these numerous potty runs are done scrupulously for two to three days, their new baby will be quickly potty trained. It goes without saying that each successful potty run is greeted with lavish praise, dancing and possibly excessive joy!

It is the new owners that have to be successfully trained first!

Chapter 15

First Three Weeks

Your ongoing fun job is praising momma and loving the babies. Your ongoing not-so-fun job is to provide clean towels all the time. There will be some natural vaginal discharge for several weeks. Occasionally your momma will miss cleaning up a poop so it is up to you to keep the bedding meticulously clean. At this time, the pups' den is the pallet of towels upon which they nurse and sleep. Now your prepared stack of towels comes into play. You can pop a clean bar rag over a messy area as an interim step to help keep the pups clean. Don't forget the cold water soak. I often begin a load of laundry in the wee hours of the morning so as not to run out of clean towels and cleaning rags.

During the first weeks you have three main jobs:

- The first job, just guess, is laundry, laundry, and more laundry.

- The second job is clipping the puppies' nails. I hate this job. I am always terrified I will trim too much and make them bleed. If that happens, it is no biggie, but I feel horrible. Clipping must be done or the pups' razor sharp nails will scratch the bitch's belly when they knead the breast while nursing. Such scratches invite infection.

- The third job is checking her tits daily.

I won't even glorify a fourth job with a number: somewhere

between the second and third week you need to worm the pups. See Chapter 21 Fleas, Worms and Shots.

Get the family and friends to handle the pups: the more handling and loving and kissing the better. This is the beginning of socialization and this wonderful playing with the pups makes them secure and confident, preparing them to enter the outside world.

The first time I took a litter of pups to the vet for their six-week Baer Hearing Test, I felt proud and accomplished as the vet and assistants all complimented me on the socialization of the pups. The veterinarian remarked "See how comfortable your pups are at being held and handled. I immediately recognize the litters that have been isolated in some back room. They stiffen up and squirm. See how calm yours are."

My grandchildren and all their friends are my secret weapon for the pups' easy attitude. The students in the private piano studio of my daughter are my second secret weapon: each student gets a puppy break. I don't think my daughter has ever threatened "No practice/no puppies!" When I shared this sentence with her she said: "Actually, I have used this threat."

What child when asked if they wanted to see some new puppies would say no? For that matter, what friend of any age when asked the same question would reply in the negative? The only limit in the number of wonderful socializers a day occurs when I tire of visitors. I am always present to protect squirming pups from being dropped and to insure that visitors follow general rules of no biting, no chewing of shoes or clothing, no jumping up and so on.

Good luck with visitors following those rules!

Chapter 16

Socialization

Socialization has already begun. I have repeatedly mentioned this vital process. Are you already tired of reading about it?

The TV spots all say talk, sing and read to your baby. The same is true of your pups. My main socializer, my granddaughter Isabella Mireles (from the time she was three years old onward), got right into the pool while the pups were nursing and read books to the pups even before their ears and eyes were open. Soon they began to crawl into her lap. Her delight was to tuck them into her shirt next to her heart.

That is why I like my litters right in the room where I live. The pups get used to activity and loud noises. Pick them up. Kiss them. They will squirm at first, but soon get used to being handled.

You now have to put on your "educator" hat. When talking to anyone expressing interest in getting a pup, you start with your Socialization Lecture. Advise your new owners to be sure to introduce the pup to different people, to other dogs for play dates and to beginning dog obedience classes. If they wait too long, they will have a pup that thinks he is a human and the pup may also become leash aggressive and/or fearful of other dogs.

The next time you talk to your prospective puppy owner repeat the entire lecture. Why? They are not ready to hear it until they are ready. Sometimes they will listen only after a behavior problem crops up. Then they just may be ready to heed your advice.

Be there for them. Their success is your success.

The vets will insist "No play dates until after all the shots."

That means no interaction for a couple of months after leaving the litter. It is too long to wait. Tell your new parents to be cautious, but arrange play dates in a safe area with other dogs that have had their shots.

This reiterated lecture on socialization helps the new puppy owner continue to guide the pup in becoming a family member who is comfortable in all situations. The result is that the new parent will sing praises of your puppies and rave to others about the temperament of their new pup. In other words, they all will be very happy!

Continued socialization is a huge key for success in the puppy's very own Forever Home. Yes, I do repeat. I am an octogenarian. I am allowed to repeat.

How many repetitions did you receive before you learned to say please and thank you?

Chapter 17

Weaning

You will need the following to start weaning the pups between their third and fourth weeks:

- Gerber Baby Rice or Oatmeal Cereal
- Canned evaporated milk or goat milk
- Puppy milk replacement (Esbilac)
- One puppy feeding bowl, stainless steel with the hump in the middle
- An electric tea kettle (optional)
- Chlorhexidine (10%) and/or vinegar and water in a spray bottle
- At least one X-pen, possibly two, to keep active pups within the pool
- Double-Headed Bolt Snaps (5 or 6 large ones to connect the X-pens)
- Larger pool depending upon the size of the mother and pups

I use an electric tea kettle to heat the metal bowl for the watered-down mixture as my faucet is far away from the hot water heater. We in Southern California cannot waste a drop waiting for the hot water to arrive at the sink. I heat the metal feeding dish (the one with the hump) first with hot water to take the chill off the metal. Dump that. Then I mix milk, cereal and Esbilac powder with hot water for a loose consistency, testing the temperature with my finger as for any baby. The resulting glop will thicken as it cools. You may have to add warm water as the puppies eat.

Get ready to video the first time they try "solid" food. They need to be hungry so don't let them nurse until later. Put momma outside or away. Remove all blankets from the pool before setting the food bowl down in the middle of the pool. Try to arrange for someone to help video this special event. It is hysterical.

I was appalled the very first time I fed a litter from the weaning bowl. Several pups literally fell into the food having no idea of what to do. For some I had to push their little faces into the gruel to give them the idea that "Hey, this tastes good!" Their paws and bodies were covered with the milky mess and it was all over the bottom of the pool. Later you may have to help some hesitant pups who cannot to push their way through the pack surrounding the food bowl. Pick up a pup, shove some others out of the way and plop the pup down in an open space in the crowded circle.

After they have eaten (if that is what you can call it), let mommy back in with the pups. She is always happy to clean little faces and bodies. She will be equally happy to polish off the remaining food in their bowl as her treat.

When they are fat tummied and sleeping in a cozy pile on clean fresh towels at the back of the pool, your work goes on. Clean the vacated pool area with your cleaning solution in an easy-to-use spray bottle. Your bar rags and handheld gripper will save your back. Don't forget to clean the feeding bowl if your bitch has left any traces of food. The stuck-on pabulum resembles a cement substitute when dried.

Finally, relax. For a first time try at weaning, ya done good!

As for frequency of feeding times, the pups will train you quickly. Eventually they will want breakfast, lunch, dinner and a late snack to hold them through the night (plus my nemesis: the early, early morning feeding). The trick is to have the food ready to go before they start loudly demanding it. You become a sneaky, tiptoeing preparer, working at top speed to avoid the clamor when they see you and know food is coming.

Be sure to get another video of all the pups, spaced out around the bowl, with no one talking in the background. The sound of their happy slurping is a unique sound you'll want to hear again. Just recalling that delightful noise makes me happy.

Make sure that slurping sound follows them throughout their lives by instructing the new owners to "float the food." This means add quite a bit of water each time the dogs are fed in order to make sure they are always well hydrated.

So Your Bitch Is Pregnant

Chapter 18

Transition Time

Dalmatians, my beloved breed, are medium-sized dogs weighing from about 45 to 70 pounds. The number of the babies they have will vary. My ladies are good breeders and generally have from eight to twelve pups each litter. As I said, the number of pups doesn't matter as momma takes care of everything for two to three good weeks. Transition time comes with weaning. Why? What goes in must come out. More is going in so more has to come out. It can get messy.

This is an interim time when you think, "Why in hell did I get into this mess?" Substitute poop for mess and you have the visual picture. The front of the pool becomes a lake of pee with little volcanoes of poop. If you aren't quick enough, they step and slide in it. It's a grim picture, sadly accurate.

My advice: Get them outside!!

If you cannot because of weather, scoop them up and plunk them into a second, pristine pen. Then you can clean up the first pen while they are working on their second mess.

I have an igloo in my yard and when the pups are about three and one half weeks old, I get up the courage to take them outside. They sleep in a pile in the igloo and are quite toasty even when the temperature at night gets as low as 40 degrees. Before I make the decision to get them outside, I go round and round in my mind about actually doing it.

"Is it too soon? What about owls and hawks? Will I still hear the pups outside my window? etc. etc."

Then I make the move and wonder why I hesitated. The pups already understand to keep their bedding in the igloo dry. And they poop in the grass. Wheeee! I am liberated as grass cleanup is easier. I even use a blast from the hose when necessary. At first they eliminate close to the igloo but eventually they find spots along the edges of the pen away from their sleeping area.

I don't know how breeders of a winter litter ever survive with a batch of pups confined inside due to the cold and snow. Even here with a tad bit of rain in Southern California I fret. I am spoiled. The pups are never happy to have to return to the inside smaller pen after experiencing the freedom of the larger back yard pen. So pray for good weather. Pups are routine driven, so if you have to put them out during the day, they are happy to come in at night as long as you do not vary the routine. Once is a habit with Dalmatians and probably also for your breed of puppies.

Success is in the consistency of routine. Isn't that just the unvarnished truth for us too?

Chapter 19

The Outside Pen

You must plan ahead for a mass puppy escape. A failsafe plan is vital if there is a dangerous area like a pool near your outside puppy pen. Always double fence. Pups will get out. They love tight spots. They dig. They escape hopefully into a safe area, flooding out to examine the inside of your house or whatever they can find that is new and exciting. Be ready: one day you will forget to hook the gate and a mad dash of inquisitive rascals will spill out into another area.

I use X-pens hooked together with Double-Headed Bolt Snaps at a height more than I can imagine the pups able to climb. A supply of these snaps is indispensible for attaching multiple X-pens together.

Unfortunately the outside pen does not mean an end to the cleanup. You can envision me garbed in plastic gloves, my box of tissues in one hand, perusing the grass for poop so that the pups can remain clean. Smooth soled shoes are a must as invariably I step in it. I hang plastic buckets at convenient intervals along the fencing to receive "the treasures" of used tissues. The smaller box of tissues works better as the plastic feeder breaks down with the jumbo size by the time you have used up about one half of the box. Then you have a wad of tissues to separate while you speedily collect the "goodies" before the pups step in them.

It is a funny sight I admit: me frantically gathering the poop while the little dears are clamoring for attention around my feet. As I try to keep them out of the mess, my "Back, Back!" and shoves help, but not much. Have the hose nearby and at the ready for that which cannot be picked up completely with one (or three) tissues.

I also hang three or four small water buckets on the bottom of the fencing so that they always have fresh water. I use the mist setting on the hose to cool them off when it is hot. The first birthing pool is now ready for water play or toy storage.

Here is a secret that took me fifteen litters to discover. When you enter the gate of the puppy pen, no matter how quick you are at squeezing sideways through the opening, one of the mob squeaks by and gets out. I finally figured out how to prevent escapees. I took a short X-pen and made a semi circle around the inside of the gate. That way I can get in, close the gate, and then step over the short X-pen. I can even lean over the low fencing and put their food down.

And this idea took me fifteen years? The best I can say in my defense is that there is a lot going on with a litter. At this point in the game I suspect that you have already discovered this fact.

Chapter 20

Early Training

Shortly after getting the litter outside between three and four weeks of age and after settling them through the first nights, my friend Susan Dalton came over to visit. She is a trainer and the owner of the California School for Dogs. She bravely sat down on the brick patio whereupon all the puppies, being their untrained selves, swamped her. Within twenty minutes, Susan had all of them not jumping up on her at all. It seemed a miracle. All she did was to pet only the pups that had four feet on the ground. They caught onto that immediately. This proves that training, like socialization, begins "yesterday."

You must guard against your visitors "Oh, I don't mind if they jump on me." Ban those from the puppy pen as that permissiveness immediately tears down the pups' good habits.

Be tough with nibbling. Actually, let's call it what it is: biting. Immediately stop thinking of them as just baby puppies who don't know any better. Don't let them bite, nibble, or mouth you. If you have a pile of toys nearby, use the substitute method of distraction with a "Here, bite on this." Otherwise there are several methods to prevent this teething habit from continuing.

The first method is for you to let out a loud, high-pitched shriek! This helps the pup make the connection that biting hurts.

The second method I call the frontal method. Wrap your thumb and index finger around the nose. Hold for about three seconds and release.

The third method, approached from the back of the head, is

to say nothing and roll the pup's upper lip over the eye tooth with your index finger and squeeze gently. This lets them bite down on their own lip and they squeal. They finally may get the picture that biting hurts. This method requires a bit of practice on your part but soon you will be doing it automatically when a pup mouths you.

All methods work if you are consistent and if you train your visitors and they are consistent. Of course, when new people arrive to play with the pups there is some slippage of discipline.

One more important no-no: make the pups leave all shoes and clothing alone. I roll the pups off my shoes rather forcefully. Forcefully is a euphemism for knocking them over! Then I tell visitors who are always reluctant to shove them firmly off their shoes "See, they don't bother mine."

My own education is constantly evolving based on the fact that puppies are extremely smart and there is no end to what they can learn. Today I learned a technique from a fabulous puppy breeder and trainer. See Chapter 25 Training Guru. New visitors to the puppy pen should "make like a statue with eyes to the sky" and allow the pups time to greet and sniff while the visitors stand woodenly. The excited pups will calm down faster without frantic shouts of "off" or "down" that won't work anyway. What a valuable new piece of training education for me!

I have mentioned this suggestion before. Resist your strong desire to take just one of the pups out of their pen and play with him or her elsewhere. My granddaughter Leah Mireles always sneaks a pup out into the living room and lavishes attention upon it. The old pen did not suffice after the pup experienced the outside world and then was put back into the small pen, exactly like that old WW I song "How ya gonna keep 'em down on the farm after they've seen Paree (Paris)?" You may have a malcontent on your hands after such an adventure, one that the little rascal will vociferously demand repeatedly.

What you can train your pups to do or not to do is almost unlimited. Your time and tons of patience is all that is needed.

More important in the earlier weeks is the lavishing of attention and love upon the pups.

Happily all of us will excel at attention, praise and love!

So Your Bitch Is Pregnant

Chapter 21

Fleas, Worms and Shots

This chapter title "Fleas, Worms and Shots" cries out for the addition of "Oh My!" Of course, check with your vet for suggestions in handling all three. Your particular breed may have other tasks.

Fleas must not be eliminated with harsh chemicals on momma or the pups. There are numerous horror stories circulating regarding bad reactions to flea medications. I have used Diatomatious Earth successfully to control fleas. Purchase the animal-grade product which is completely natural. Basically it is a white powder made from ground up ancient sea creatures, used commercially for filtering systems in pools. This fine powder coats the fleas and smothers them and is safe for both mommas and for puppies. Hurrah!

My morning routine is to slap on my baseball cap for sun protection, give the adult dogs a happy "Let's pick up the poop," and immediately after that chore I give them all a brushing and very slight dusting of the powder whereupon they all get a spoonful of organic coconut oil as a reward. The brush-dust-coconut oil treatment does wonders for their coats. If I find fleas on the puppies, they get a very light dusting too.

Worms are another matter entirely. There will be minimum worms in the pups if you were foresighted enough to worm your bitch before impregnation. Don't even consider worming her if she is pregnant. Even if you did worm her before impregnation, it is still almost impossible to eliminate all worms because of the varied cycles always present in the bitch. Check with your vet as to what worming medicine is recommended to use on the puppies. I use a plastic syringe to suck up the yellow liquid to the directed amount on the bottle of Nemex-2. Slip the tip into the side of the side of the mouth and express slowly. The pups think it is delicious!

Prepare yourself. Nursing mothers invariably have worms. Vermicelli will never look the same to you again after worming your pups. If you utter a horrified "Ugh," you are in for it. If you think to yourself: "Good, look at all those nasty worms we killed," you are in for an exciting time. Dead and still wiggling ones will appear in about four to six hours after giving worm medicine to the pups. More worms will continue to show up for about a day. This worming task is done every two to three weeks. No way around it as some stage or other is ingested from the mother's milk. Once with a particularly bad infestation, I had a pup that actually barfed up several live worms. Now that was a double "Ugh." I raced to the shelf holding the worming liquid.

Worms are part of it's all natural that we don't appreciate.

Shots are a breeze by comparison. Some vets will give the first shots at six weeks while others want to wait until eight weeks. Many breeders give their own shots. I am not one of them. I like to combine the hearing test, first shots and microchipping in one fell swoop with the pups' first vet visit. Microchipping is mandated for the Baer Hearing Test for Dalmatians. If Microchipping is not required for your breed to register test results, you may be able to leave that task for your new owner to accomplish.

The hardest part of getting shots is rounding up all the pups, putting them in the car, going to the vet and returning without barf and poop all over the pups and the car. Lots of towels over plastic will help.

After that first visit to the vet, give yourself a hearty "Good job, puppy momma!"

Chapter 22

The Contract

Why have a contract? Both you as breeder as well as the new puppy owner need to be protected. You provided a healthy pet and the pup's perfect health should be collaborated within 48 hours by a vet chosen by the new owner. The new exam also provides a base for obtaining pet insurance on the new puppy.

There should be some kind of return policy in the contract. If you have heard of the phrase "buyer's remorse" regarding the terror of a new homeowner, consider the possible what-have-I-done attitude of the new owner after the pup has howled relentlessly the first nights away from the litter. In addition the pup may have already peed and chewed on their prized Oriental rug. My contract has a hefty fee for a returned puppy to deter the immediate shock of puppy noise and possible destruction. I have never had to invoke such a fine, but just like the chapter "Money Matters," you must be clear as to your return policy to ensure a forever home. A written contract provides a sound base from which you can negotiate what is best for all involved.

I heaved a sigh of relief that Friday morning after the last pup in a litter of twelve was placed in a crate in the back of a large SUV to go to his new home. The new owner was a young person who had diligently saved up the price for the new pup. She had researched the breed and had owned dogs previously. I had explained the contract thoroughly and she had signed it and given me the full price for the pup in cash. The one previous hesitation in my mind about her getting the pup was that her younger sister was going to come and live with her. In my mind it was a lot of responsibility for a young lady who was going to college and working part time. However, her experience and determination convinced me that the pup would be adored. I kissed the pup and gave her a hug. I returned to my office to call a gentleman who had indicated an interest in the same pup to tell him that the pup had been placed. He was disappointed but understood. I was happy that the last pup of the large litter was placed.

People often say "I could never breed as I wouldn't be able to part with the puppies." After ten to twelve weeks of round the clock work, midnight and five A.M. feedings, cleaning, socializing, loving, I predict you will be ready for a puppy break.

Less than five minutes after she left with the puppy the doorbell rang. She had driven the pup approximate four blocks. The pup must have been howling the entire time. In a distraught voice she said: "I can't do this you have to take the pup back." All I could think of was that I had just cut off my last possible owner. Then I shouted through her distress "Yes, you can. You are having a panic attack." I marched her back to the SUV and the howling puppy telling her repeatedly "Yes you can do this! You will keep the pup at least for the weekend and after the weekend if you still don't want him, we will talk." I explained that of course he would cry in a new situation away from his littermates for the first time.

All that afternoon I debated whether or not to call her to check on how things were going. Finally late that afternoon I telephoned. She had driven directly to a local pet shop for supplies where everyone gave her tons of attention about her darling pup. She had played with him outside in her yard and settled him in the house for a nap. It was all okay. Later I learned that the bond the two girls had with the puppy really helped their home situation.

So get a signed contract. You can then decide from a position of strength to do what is best for all involved. Following is a copy of the contract I use. Feel free to utilize it as a guide and modify in any way to make it your own.

The Contract

FYREHOUSE DALMATIANS

Contract and Condition of Sale for AKC Quality Pet

Buyer Information:

Ginger & Jim Smith

1627 Georgetown Street

Lafayette, LA 70506

whateveremail@cox.net

(439) 961-7513

Seller Information:

Eleanor Winters

6167 Craigmont Drive

Goleta, CA 93117

eleanorwinters@cox.net

(805) 964-5911

Date of Sale:	June 24, 2017
Purchase Price:	$1900.00
Breed of Dog:	Dalmatian
Color:	(B/W or liver) Black and White
Name of Dog:	Fyrehouse N Xanadu's Phyllis/Ellie
Sex:	Female
Data of Birth:	June 20, 2017
Place of Birth:	Goleta, CA
Litter Reg. No:	NP465599

Sire: AKC: NM9999999   CH Daisydot Checker Flag (aka Desoto)

Dam: AKC: NP44444444   Fyrehouse Betty Davis Eyes

This dog is a purebred, pedigreed Dalmatian. This dog can be registered with the AKC.

Should you decide to breed this dog/bitch, the breeder will be consulted and approval given or withheld.

Provided this dog is returned to the above Seller (henceforth referred to as "Breeder") with a signed statement from a licensed veterinarian, the Breeder agrees to a cash refund or replacement upon the following condition: At the option and expense of the buyer, this dog will be taken to a licensed veterinarian for a thorough health examination within 48 hours from the time of delivery to the buyer. A licensed veterinarian must confirm the prognosis before the dog can be returned at the expense of the buyer.

Replacement (if available) Option: Yes. If for any reason the return procedure is not completed (or fulfilled) within the designated time agreed upon, the buyer agrees to pay the seller $1900.00 USD for the cost of replacement of the dog in his/her line of breeding.

If, at some future date, the buyer does not wish to keep the dog, it is to be returned to the seller with an additional charge of $1000.00 for failure to complete and/or fulfill the above listed contract/agreement.

All fees involved must be paid in full before AKC papers will be released to new owner.

Should the buyer at any later time be unable to keep the dog in question, the buyer will contact the Breeder (Eleanor Green Winters) and:

1) Return the dog to the Breeder or 2) Transfer the dog to a new owner who has been approved by the Breeder. Such approval will not be unreasonably withheld, providing that the new owner also be bound by the provisions of this contract.

Any deletions to this contract shall be struck out and initialed by both parties. No other warrantees or guarantees, expressed or implied, is made under this contract.

I acknowledge this understanding and accept all the conditions of this contract as indicated by my signature below.

Signed:

Buyer: _____   Date: _____
                 Jim & Ginger Smith

Breeder: _____   Date: _____
                 Eleanor Green Winters

Chapter 23

Insurance

I never thought I would be writing about insurance. My dad always claimed (unintended pun) that he planned to form an insurance business that would pay if your first insurance company denied the claim. If they didn't pay, his would. Now there was a moneymaker for sure...

Since we all hope that the need for vet care will not occur and definitely don't want another insurance bill, I am surprised that I now suggest to new puppy owners that they get health insurance for their pup.

Dogs can't say "It hurts here." The source of discomfort requires tests that pet insurance providers generally cover if your vet recommends them. However, vet insurance companies have "pre-existing" clauses. The trick is to be insured before the first badly cut paw, before the eating of a stuffed toy which blocks the intestines or before a bout of continuing diarrhea. Murphy's Law is invariably in effect when all these problems arise at night or on the weekend.

Check out several pet insurance companies. Some offer various deductible levels which may fit into your monthly budget. Policies usually have a two-week waiting period before the insurance kicks in, so be sure to get a clean bill of health from your puppy's vet before you apply for insurance. Of course, read carefully about all the exclusions.

Never ignore the marvelous benefit of peace of mind that comes with insurance. Many owners wait far too long to go to their vet as they dread the expense. That fear is minimized when you have insurance. Yes, you pay monthly and there is also a yearly deductible, but the amount will not be as catastrophic as it would be without insurance.

Honestly I was guilty of waiting too long to take my Phoebe in to be treated with the mastitis I have already described. I knew it would be at least $1000 to $1500 that I did not have at the time. And, yes, it was a weekend when I realized I could wait no longer. One breeder I know insists in the contract that each pup be insured by the new owner so that there will be no hesitation in getting treatment based on monetary fears. Frankly, that is a damn good idea that I intend to push with new puppy owners.

However anything to do with canine pregnancy and whelping usually is not covered by insurance.

Hummm.

Sexist discrimination?

Chapter 24

The Alpha

Dogs are pack animals. If you don't establish yourself from the get-go as the alpha, the puppy will immediately assume that position. It doesn't matter if the puppy is a tiny Yorkie or a huge Mastiff. Locally there is a well-known trainer, Joe Martinez, who asks one question of a prospective client and refuses to accept them as clients if that question is answered with a yes. That question is "Do you let your dog on the bed or couch?"

Think back on all the ancestral wolf pictures you have seen. The alpha male or female is always depicted upon a higher hill than the rest of the pack. Height is a position of dominance. After the pup is trained in basic obedience, it may be okay to allow them up on furniture or beds when they are invited. Otherwise, you lose. If you are not the alpha, that pup will fill the void.

Commanding the alpha position does not mean that you are harsh or abusive. It is a comfort to the dog to know his place in the family. The rules you establish don't matter either. It is simply that you are the alpha and you establish the rules, not the dog.

But it is not all gloom and doom as your new pup's main desire is to please you. Positive reinforcement is the term for going crazy with love and praise for good behavior. If they like a treat, give them a jackpot of two or three treats plus love for especially good behavior. Next time maybe give only one treat with praise. The time after that give them no treat, just love. They will always "come" or respond to the command as they are not sure how great the reward will be.

Training classes are really to train the new puppy owner coupled with socialization with other dogs of all sizes and shapes. As a breeder, you cannot control the new home environment. Owners call for help usually after the bad behavior is established. One or two might attempt to shift the blame of puppy problems onto your pedigree or lack thereof. Eventually they may have to pay for professional help to correct a bad habit they allowed. All you can do is to repeat and point out to them that when the puppy left, you gave them a large folder containing several printouts: vet records, signed contract, pedigree if there is one, diet and training suggestions, etc.

"Awwww, how adorable he is jumping up to give me a hug and kiss!" Be careful what you allow in the name of cuteness. A puppy galloping about in greeting is one thing. A 65 pound adult canine is another. That adorable little yip for attention may be charming at first, but when it blossoms into insistent barking? Make one guess as to whom to blame in both scenarios.

Once is a habit with my Dalmatians. Perhaps your breed also remembers your early training hiccups for a very long time?

Chapter 25

Training Guru

One night I saw a video on Facebook of seven Dalmatian pups seated in a semicircle around their breeder, each accepting a treat gently, one by one. The video literally blew me away as the pups were only seven weeks old! I have mentioned how teachable little puppies are but I am quite satisfied when I can go into the puppy pen and have the pups leave my shoes and clothing alone and refrain from jumping up on me. I stand in awe of what this breeder has accomplished with her training.

I immediately sent a private message to Karen Rowan about her spectacular accomplishment and asked her to call me as I wished to hear how she did this feat. I told her I would add a chapter giving her complete credit. So far we haven't been able to connect. I know I am looking for the magic solution.

If you have pups with confirmation show potential, some suggest that you do not teach them to sit at first. That comes later. Instead initially teach them the down command. A possible show puppy is one that has all the requisites: excellent temperament (top priority in my book), health, structure, movement and markings etc. However, puppies have an astounding ability to learn many commands and can easily distinguish the difference between the command to sit and the command to stand. Training one puppy at a time is doable. But training seven or more bouncing puppies is amazingly difficult.

I appreciate Karen's remarkable success. A pack of puppies feed off of each other and control is almost impossible. I want her "open sesame" secret to that control. Of course, in my heart I know it is tons of training time with consistent repetition. I still hope that there is a quick fix I have overlooked.

Karen just posted another video of her pups. This time she is introducing them to swimming in a 93 degree hot tub. She has each one in a little puppy life jacket and gently puts them one at a time into the hot tub and gives them treats as they swim. They love it. Forget me: get a puppy from her! You will have little to do to train a puppy from her as the pup she provides will already be taught the basics and more.

As soon as I get her "open sesame," I will definitely let you know about it. However, I don't have to hear from her to know that there are no quick fixes for training.

Damn.

P.S. I just heard from Karen. As I thought, there are no prestos. However there is hope for all of us as she is planning to write a book on puppy training.

Hurrah!

Chapter 26

Ongoing

This chapter labeled "Ongoing" is actually an epilogue regarding the new lives of your pups.

Many new owners will become dear friends. Some will disappear into the woodwork and you will not hear from them. But most will regale you with Christmas pictures and reports of the delightful antics of their puppy, right on through the years, expressing their gratitude for such a marvelous family member.

These ongoing vignettes are the fun part. The reflected love and delight in their puppy is generously thrown back to you, literally bathing you with love and attention for your good work. This sounds pretty flowery, but it is really why anyone has a litter: to share this unstinting love.

To paraphrase what Eckhart Tolle asserts in his lovely little book Guardians of Being: all dogs (and cats) bring us into the now of life. They bring us into presence. Dogs eat, sleep, run and play wholeheartedly in the now, not like us who multitask our way through life on iphones and ipads. Enough philosophy, but just observe. Animals are so very here and now and at hand, plus they always epitomize the unconditional love for which we strive.

May I end this little book on one final thought? Bless yourselves for helping add so much love with your litter of puppies for families, for the world and maybe even for the universe.

Good on you!

So Your Bitch Is Pregnant

Acknowledgements

The phrase "It takes a village to raise a child"
is true for puppies as well!

I want to thank my friends and especially my long-suffering family, all of whom refrained from obvious eye rolls when I launched into my puppy stories.

My family audience also contributed to endless "how-do-I-do-this" regarding computer and internet tasks. For repeated assistance, I thank grandchildren Nora, Leah and Nino Mireles as competent wizards on the computer. The younger grandchildren (JJ Winters and Isabella Mireles) excelled at puppy socialization, Isa having grown up with generations of Dalmatians in her delighted embrace. My daughter Jessica Mireles added her private piano students with weekly "puppy breaks" as their reward for quality practicing.

My extended "Dalmatian" family I thank with citations sprinkled throughout this book. They fill the journey with encouragement and appreciation. Dennis Sanders (mentor, friend and guru of our team) is the dear friend to whom I dedicate this book.

Lastly, I commend Bo von Hohenlohe, webmaster and book-producer, for his patience with my octogenarian technical struggles as well as his encouragement regarding this legacy/memoir of my 17 year career.

I also thank you, the reader, delighted puppy momma or papa, and trust that you also will love the journey.

Addendum

Choosing Your Puppy

Male or Female: which is better?

Neither is better. Both are wonderful. However, there are plusses and minuses on both sides.

Females used to be avoided as new owners did not wish to deal with the seasonal problem: bitches usually have two "heat cycles" each year, beginning approximately at seven to nine months. Now most owners opt to have females spayed before their first heat to avoid the problem entirely. Somehow, I am not convinced about the safety of early spaying in females. There may be health repercussions of too early spaying of females. One should research this topic to make sure you act in the best interest of your new little girl.

Males, of course, are exempt from the problem of the seasonal "periods." However, there is a fight in 2019 over the best time to neuter a male in order to prevent "marking" (the term for lifting the leg to pee onto furniture etc.) or for male-to-male aggression problems as the dog matures. The current thought from accomplished breeders and some veterinarians is that you should wait until 18 to 20 months before neutering a male. Males need the hormones, particularly testosterone, for proper bone growth until about 20 months: another subject of study for the new puppy owner.

As for temperament considerations of male versus female, I feel that it is totally an individual prospect. Some males are laid back and gentle as are some females. In both genders you will also find some active and feisty pups. Be sure you make clear to the breeder which traits in a puppy you prefer.

Early socialization and consistent training of your pup can help your pup arrive somewhere "in the middle" between active and laid back.

Puppy Suggestions

New puppy parents have lots of questions. Here are a few suggestions (based upon my 17 litters) that you need to know right away. Of course, your individual vet may have further instructions which you may choose (or not choose) to follow.

Shots and Testing

All puppies of the litter of June 20, 2017, have received the Baer Hearing Test on August 4, 2017; all were microchipped and received their first set of puppy shots at the same time (the second set of shots should be given by your vet based on the date of the first shots); all pups passed the Baer Test with bilateral (i.e. perfect) hearing! Although all pups have been wormed many times, you will need to worm them at least once more. Your vet can supply you with worming etc. medication. You will receive a contract which requires that you visit your vet for a complete exam (for our respective protection) within 48 hours of receiving your pup.

Food

I now use Nutro Max Lamb and Rice Large Breed Puppy Food. Soak it so it is soft and add rice and pumpkin if poops are not firm. I add a little of some grain free mix to the food of the older dogs. Choose a fairly high protein count for the pups for the first six months or so. After six months, keep the protein content much lower (21 to 25 %) if you can. I am now using Purina ProPlan Select for Sensitive Stomachs and Skins with Salmon (whew, a long one). This can be purchased at PetSmart or Petco. It is expensive, but they like it. Sometimes I add a spoonful of canned meat, yogurt, chicken, vegetables, egg, whatever (probably more for my eye than theirs). Careful. It always looks like not-enough-food-to-our-eyes, and in a flash, you will have a pudgy Dalmatian. If that happens, feed a little less dry food each feeding until you like the look.

My girls get 3/4 cup of dry food in the morning and 3/4 cup at night plus whatever additives I choose. I also give them each a dollop of solid coconut oil when I brush them in the morning. It does wonders for their coats. You will have to discover your favorite mixes. Remember always to switch foods gradually so their stomachs will not be upset by the change.

Purines

As you know, Dalmatians sometimes form crystals or stones in their urine. The problem is in the breed. Do not feed your Dalmatian any beef or organ meats! The problem is worse for the males because of their "plumbing." My theory is that a low protein diet dry food, PLENTY of water, and a TON of exercise, prevents this problem. Your vet can give a urine test at a regular visit. An ultrasound for the males is a better way to check for crystals. I am also sending a Purine Chart so you can see which foods are a big no-no for Dalmatians.

Vitamins

I use NuVet Plus, one tablet daily, for my adults. I credit Folly's (the Fyrehouse matriarch) longevity to this product. She lived to be 14. Great Grandma Olivia is 13 and doing well. I will send you a letter re the benefits of NuVet Plus. You may order by calling (800) 474-7044 (ask for Josh---he is great) with the Order Code: 69217. Or you may click on the NuVet Plus "bottle" at the bottom of the home page for www.fyrehousedalmatians.com. The pups are already getting ¼ to ½ tablet every day since week six.

Crate Training

This is a wonderful help: the crate is their den, hideaway, comfort zone, refuge etc. In addition, the crate keeps the pup safe and your stuff intact when you cannot pay attention.

Keep the crate small at first. Use a cardboard box to block off the back half of the crate if you have purchased a large crate anticipating the growth of your pup. Possibly cover the crate with a blanket to make it even more den-like. As the pup doesn't like to soil the bed, there will not be enough room to potty if you keep it snug. Place the crate near your bed at first as whining usually indicates the pup needs to go out and you need to hear "the request."

Those first nights can be a little rough. Being in a new home with no siblings can be scary. You have to tough it out with them the first few nights. Soon, hopefully, they will be sleeping when you do! Kongs with food or treats inside help when you have to leave them crated during the day, never more than two or three hours at a time. The rule of thumb is one hour for each month of age, ending at about four hours max.

Potty Training

The pups already try to potty near their fence line. Be diligent the first two to three days. Take the pup on the leash to the spot where you want him to go, wait, wait, and WAIT, and make a huge deal when the pup potties: praise, smile, treat him. Again, make a big deal. This potty break must be done each time the pup changes activity! You are the one that has to be trained the first couple of days!! If you do this correctly, your pup should immediately be potty trained. Yep, I promise. However, it is up to you. If they have an accident, don't say anything, just take them where they should go, wait, praise, and clean up later.

Socialization

Get your pup with many different people AND dogs. If you wait too long to introduce the pup to other dogs (some vets make owners wait until all shots are done), the pup will think he is a person and be fearful or fear-aggressive toward other dogs. Puppy classes, puppy play dates. dog day care etc. are invaluable in furthering the socialization I have already accomplished with the pups. If you vet says "Wait," find another dog that has his shots and make a play date. These are the basic things I think you should know immediately. The general rule of training is POSITIVE RE-INFORCEMENT. They want to please you. Ignore the incorrect (as best as you can), distract, and reward the good. REWARD THE GOOD with praise and small treats.

Remember two things from this lengthy epistle:

1. Picture that "cute thing" the puppy does and imagine having a 50/60-pound Dalmatian doing the same thing.

2. Remember: ONCE is a habit for a Dalmatian!

Enjoy and call me with any questions. I will be there for you. Eleanor Green Winters (805) 964-5911 cell: (805)-689-4081 or eleanorwinters@cox.net

Invoice

Sample Invoice

VETERINARY MEDICAL CENTER
8165 MORRO ROAD, STE A-B-C
ATASCADERO, CA 93422
(805) 461-3002

The Standard of
Veterinary Excellence
AAHA
ACCREDITED

Client ID: 9791
Invoice #: 156460
Date: 4/18/2016

ELEANOR WINTERS
6167 CRAIGMONT DR.
GOLETA, CA 93117

| Patient ID: 9791-3 | Species: CANINE | Weight: | |
| Patient Name: PHOEBE | Breed: DALMATIAN | Birthday: 07/10/2011 | Sex: Female |

	Description	Staff Name	Quantity	Total
4/18/2016	BAER HEARING TEST	Dr. B. Hollstien	12.00	$540.00
	FIRST PUPPY VACCINATION		12.00	$204.00
	INSERT OWN MICROCHIP		12.00	$132.00
	BNP Ophthalmic Ointment		1.00	$20.00
			Patient Subtotal:	**$896.00**

Instructions
A FEW PETS MAY EXPERIENCE SOME LETHARGY AND SORENESS FROM THE VACCINATIONS. IF THIS
PERSISTS LONGER THAN 24 HOURS, PLEASE CALL OUR OFFICE.

Reminder
09/04/2015   2ND PUPPY VACCINATION
05/09/2016   2ND PUPPY VACCINATION

Invoice Total:	**$896.00**
Total:	$896.00
Invoice Balance Due:	$896.00
VISA Card Number: ...XXXX9217:	($896.00)
Less Payment:	($896.00)
Invoice Balance Due:	**$0.00**
Balance Due:	**$0.00**

In case of emergency outside our business hours, you may contact the Atascadero
Pet Emergency Hospital at 805-466-3880.

NuVet Letter

Dear Puppy Buyer,

I highly recommend NuVet Plus.

More than a million dogs and cats are using NuVet to **protect against most ailments** (from back yard pesticides, pet food allergies and hormones, toxic formaldehyde in furniture and carpeting, ailments transmitted from dog parks and the vet's office, etc), while maintaining a **beautiful skin and coat**.

This is not just a vitamin. It's an **immune system builder** with a precise balance of vitamins, minerals, omega fatty acids, amino acids and high-potency antioxidants. That's why it works so well through all three stages of a dog's life.

- ✓ **For younger dogs** (under 2 years old), it strengthens their immune system, while building and strengthening the cardiovascular, skeletal and nerve systems.

- ✓ **For dogs in their prime** (age 2-8), it improves the luster of their skin and coat while protecting against allergies, skin and coat problems, staining from tears, digestive problems, etc.

- ✓ **For older dogs** (over 8 years old), it helps reduce and eliminate arthritis, tumors, premature aging, cataracts, heart conditions, diabetes and many types of cancer, while extending the life and improving the vitality of many dogs.

We highly recommend NuVet Plus to keep your pet on the path to perfect health! It's not available in stores, and is only available to the general public with an order code from an authorized pet professional.

For your convenience, you may order directly from the manufacturer (at up to 50% off what most veterinarians charge) by **calling 800-474-7044** and using **Order Code: 69217** or ordering **online** at **www.nuvet.com/69217** . By using autoship you can save an additional 15%.

To the long life and health of your puppy!

Eleanor Winters
Fyrehouse Dalmatians

So Your Bitch Is Pregnant

A Few Words About Dog Shows

There are tons of events to show off your wondrous puppy, to train your pup, to find new friends, to get exercise and attention and plain just have fun. Google "Fun Things to do with Your Dog."

Many of the activities are sports where the amateur can compete successfully with the professional while competing with other canines to a breed standard (more internet work for you to check the myriad of possibilities).

My experience has been with American Kennel Club (AKC) Shows in Confirmation. The judge is grounded in breed standards and judges each dog according to the breed standard in his individual mind. This is why, for instance, a Dalmatian can be judged along side of a Boston Terrier, a Pug, a Bulldog, a Poodle etc. in one of eight types of dogs grouped for similarities.

Wait: A Bulldog vs a Poodle? The breeds you have listed are totally different? That is because the group labeled "Non-Sporting" is a catchall: not a Terrier, not a Toy, not a Working Dog. It is mishmash, left-over group. The dog judged closest to its own breed standard by the presiding judge becomes the winner.

Or one can hope.

You can see the process is very open to individual interpretation and rife for mental hair pulling by the competitors. The entire event can be a "Whoopie, we won" or a lesson in being a good loser with a lottery mentality to try again. By lottery mentality I mean you have to enter: "You can't win unless you buy a ticket."

All organizations have their own "in" groups which change over time. My stock phrase for any of these competitions is "You go for the hotdog." That means you enter for fun, hope for the best, and if you don't win, enjoy the outing with your pup and eat a hotdog (at shows, they are generally very delicious). Sometimes you might feel like screaming the hell with good sportsmanship. Try to look at a loss, fair or unfair in your mind, like a lesson in patience and acceptance.

If you have ever seen the movie "Best in Show," you will think all dog show participants are loonies and certifiably insane.

We are.

Once I met and chatted with a judge on break, having a cigarette (still ok some places). She said she had given a first-time competitor her first blue ribbon for a class win. She told the newbie "This ribbon is worth $200,000!" The new owner handling her dog for the first time was aghast.

"What do you mean?" she stammered.

The judge replied that she would enter more and larger shows, need a wheeled crate for her pup to ease transportation, want umbrella and chair for hot outdoor competitions, need a bigger vehicle, travel to other states and thus probably eventually need a motor home and maybe even want to breed her winner!

In other words, she was hooked! There is the thrill like it's your kid acting in a play or musical recital, all encompassing and addicting.

There are worse addictions, yes?

A Word About Breeding

If you have read this little book, you know already that I am incapable of "just a word..."

Actually, my "word" is really a question. Why is there antagonism between good breeders and good rescuers? We both dedicate ourselves to the mutual goal of finding good homes for all dogs. We need to work together and help each other for our common purpose.

The Good

There are dedicated breeders doing their best to follow breed standards for breeding and health, for good temperament and for beauty: they research pedigrees; they do extensive testing; they socialize the pups thoroughly; and they scrutinize the prospective parents of their pups.

There are caring rescue groups and shelters: they help all animals in distress; they assist families to find suitable animals for adoption; and they, too, examine prospective owners for suitability.

The Bad

Many breeders claim that some rescue organizations are scams: "There are numerous horrible pictures of starving or injured dogs needing to be saved by your dollars, money that finds its way into the pockets of those 'begging' for cash, not into reputable facilities for the needy animals."

Many rescue groups advertise: "Some breeders are puppy mills or uninformed 'backyard breeders' producing a flood of unwanted pups in our shelters."

The Ugly

The subject of breeding versus rescue is fraught with controversy, misstatements and prejudices on both sides. Money and politics in all walks of life, yes? Some rescue groups are fraudulent; some breeders are totally in it for a quick turnaround. The entire issue is subject to continued harangue between those who breed and those who rescue.

Unfortunately, it is impossible to legislate responsibility upon either side.

You, the individual considering having a litter (if you are not already facing an "oops" litter), must ask yourself: "Why to I want to breed my bitch?" or "Why do I want to allow my dog to father a litter?"

There are many answers to contemplate, which are neither good nor bad assuming you accept totally the upcoming responsibility for the offspring.

When The Time Comes...

When choosing the "most darling puppy in the world," we rarely consider the sad fact that our pup will be with us such a short time. Large breeds only live eight to ten years. Toy breeds may live up to seventeen years or more.

There is a lovely story going around about the little boy who knew why dogs live such relatively short lives. You might wish to Google it: Why Dogs Don't Live as long as Humans (A Young Boy's Perspective).

Nor should we indulge in such unhappy reflections when viewing puppies.

Those of us who have had numerous canines in our lives know that the time will come when we have to be tough and make that sad decision. No one can tell you when that moment comes: the moment when you decide for them "that's enough."

Be tough. Be kind. Don't make your sweetheart suffer horribly and go through horrendous and possibly useless medical practices because you cannot face life without your beloved companion.

And, be with them. Yes, even when it is the worst thing you've ever had to face.

Don't let your first dog be the learning experience you need to have with euthanasia to do the right thing. Most vets and their staff know exactly what to do and to say in order to help both you and your dog. The procedure can be a loving process and actually peaceful.

However, I am tearing up just thinking about it.

It is sad. Be strong.

It is the right thing to do.

Notes

Notes

Notes

Notes

Notes

Notes

Notes

Notes

Notes

Notes

Notes

Notes

Notes

Notes

Notes

Notes

Manufactured by Amazon.ca
Bolton, ON